Daily Christian Living

with

John Henry Newman

*All booklets are published thanks to the
generous support of the members of the
Catholic Truth Society*

CATHOLIC TRUTH SOCIETY
PUBLISHERS TO THE HOLY SEE

Contents

∞

To the end of the longest life
you are still a beginner.[1]

∞

Our Christian Vocation

My vocation in life

God has created me to do him some definite
service; he has committed some work to me
which he has not committed to another. I have my
mission - I never may know it in this life, but I shall
he told it in the next. Somehow I am necessary for
his purposes, as necessary in my place as an
archangel in his - if, indeed, I fail, he can raise
another as he could make the stones children of
Abraham. Yet I have a part in this great work; I am a
link in a chain, a bond of connection between
persons. He has not created me for naught. I shall do
good, I shall do his work; I shall be an angel of
peace, a preacher of truth in my own place, while
not intending it, if I do but keep his commandments
and serve him in my calling.[2]

Complete trust in God's ways

Therefore I will trust him. Whatever, wherever I
am, I can never be thrown away. If I am in
sickness, my sickness may serve him; in perplexity,

my perplexity may serve him; if I am in sorrow, my sorrow may serve him... He does nothing in vain; he may prolong my life, he may shorten it; he knows what he is about. He may take away my friends, he may throw me among strangers, he may make me feel desolate, make my spirits sink, hide the future from me - still he knows what he is about.[3]

Submit to the loving will of God

Be sure that many others besides you feel that sadness, that years pass away and no opening comes to them for serving God... One must submit oneself to God's loving will - and be quieted by faith that what he wills for us is best. He has no need of us - he only asks for our good desires.[4]

God calls us again and again

For in truth we are not called once only, but many times; all through our life Christ is calling us. He called us first in baptism; but afterwards also. Whether we obey his voice or not, he graciously calls us still... He calls us on from grace to grace, and from holiness to holiness, while life is given us. Abraham was called from his home, Peter from his

nets, Matthew from his office,... we are all in course
of calling, on and on, from one thing to another,
having no resting-place, but mounting towards our
eternal rest, and obeying one command only to have
another put upon us. He calls us again and again, in
order to justify us again and again - and again and
again, and more and more, to sanctify and glorify us.[5]

Christ says to me everyday: follow me

It were well if we understood this, but we are slow
to master the great truth, that Christ is, as it were,
walking among us, and by his hand, or eye, or voice,
bidding us follow him. We do not understand that
his call is a thing which takes place now. We think it
took place in the apostles' days, but we do not
believe in it, we do not look out for it in our own
case. We have not eyes to see the Lord; far different
from the beloved apostle, who knew Christ even
when the rest of the disciples knew him not. When
he stood on the shore after his resurrection, and
bade them cast the net into the sea, "that disciple
whom Jesus loved saith unto Peter, "It is the Lord.""[6]

It is God who leads us

We cannot have everything in this world but we can have the greatest of all, God's presence, God's guidance. May you have it abundantly, wherever you are, and you will, but you must leave yourself in his hands who loves you.[7]

God knows what is best for us

Let us put ourselves into his hands, and not be startled though he leads us by a strange way, a *mirabilis via*, as the Church speaks. Let us be sure he will lead us right, that he will bring us to that which is not indeed what we think best, nor what is best for another, but what is best for us.[8]

Having the faith of Abraham

Abraham seems to have had something very noble and magnanimous about him. He could realize and make present to him things unseen. He followed God in the dark as promptly, as firmly, with as cheerful a heart, and bold a stepping, as if he were in broad daylight. There is something very great in this; and, therefore, St Paul calls Abraham our father, the father of Christians as well as Jews. For we are especially bound to walk by faith, not by sight; and are blessed in faith, and justified by faith, as was faithful Abraham.[9]

How can I become perfect?

In a higher world it is otherwise, but here below to live is to change, and to be perfect is to have changed often.[10]

Never standing still

If Christianity be an universal religion, suited not simply to one locality or period, but to all times and places, it cannot but vary in its relations and dealings towards the world around it, that is, it will develop.[11]

God alone is constant

Life passes, riches fly away, popularity is fickle, the senses decay, the world changes, friends die. One alone is constant; one alone is true to us; one alone can be true; one alone can be all things to us.[12]

A faithful God who never changes

All below heaven changes; spring, summer, autumn, each has its turn. The fortunes of the world change; what was high, lies low; what was low, rises high. Riches take wing and flee away; bereavements happen. Friends become enemies and enemies friends. Our wishes, aims and plans change. There is nothing stable but thou, O my God! And thou art the centre and life of all who change, who trust thee as their Father, who look to thee, and who are content to put themselves into thy hands.[13]

Only faith endures in changing times

Opinions change, conclusions are feeble, enquiries run their course, reason stops short, but faith alone reaches to the end, faith only endures.[14]

Be Faithful in Little Things

Let your yes be yes

That a thing is true is no reason that it should be said, but that it should be done; that it should be acted upon; that it should be made our own inwardly.[15]

Little acts of love

One little deed, done against natural inclination for God's sake, though in itself of a conceding or passive character, to brook an insult, to face a danger, or to resign an advantage, has in it a power outbalancing all the dust and chaff of mere profession.[16]

Actions speak louder than words

Beware lest your religion be one of feeling merely, not of practice... Many a man likes to be religious in graceful language; he loves religious tales and hymns, yet is never the better Christian for all this. The works of everyday, these are the tests of our glorious contemplations, whether or not they shall be available to our salvation; and he who does one deed of obedience for Christ's sake, let him have no imagination and no fine feeling, is a better man, and returns to his home justified rather than the most eloquent speaker and the most sensitive hearer, if such men do not practise up to their knowledge.[17]

⌒

Does what you believe make a difference?

I really fear that most men called Christians, whatever they may profess, whatever they may think they feel, whatever warmth and illumination and love they may claim as their own, yet would go on almost as they do, neither much better nor much worse, if they believed Christianity to be a fable.[18]

⌒

Find God in the ordinary things of each day

The Christian will feel that the true contemplation of his Saviour lies in his worldly business; that as Christ is seen in the poor, in the persecuted, and in children, so he is seen in the employments which he puts upon his chosen, whatever they be; that in attending to his own calling he will be meeting Christ; that if he neglect it, he will not on that account enjoy his presence at all the more, but that while performing it, he will see Christ revealed to his soul amid the ordinary actions of the day, as a sort of sacrament.[19]

⌒

Humility in everything for Christ

True faith teaches us to do numberless disagreeable things for Christ's sake, to bear petty annoyances, which we find written down in no book. In most books Christian conduct is made grand, elevated and splendid; so that anyone, who only knows of true religion from books, and not from actual endeavours to be religious, is sure to be offended at religion when he actually comes upon it, from the roughness and humbleness of his duties, and his necessary deficiencies in doing them. It is beautiful in a picture to wash the disciples' feet; but the sands of the real desert have no comeliness in them to compensate for the servile nature of the occupation.[20]

Love one another

Society gets on, and a family gets on, by a refined system of mutual concession.[21]

The sure road to perfection

It is the saying of holy men that, if we wish to be perfect, we have nothing more to do than to perform the ordinary duties of the day well. A short road to perfection - short, not because easy, but because pertinent and intelligible. There are no short ways to perfection, but there are sure ones. I think this is an instruction which may be of great practical use to persons like ourselves. It is easy to have vague ideas what perfection is, which serve well enough to talk about, when we do not intend to aim at it; but as soon as a person really desires and sets about seeking it himself he is dissatisfied with anything but what is tangible and clear, and constitutes some sort of direction towards the practice of it.[22]

Know your weakness

We must bear in mind what is meant by perfection. It does not mean any extraordinary service, anything out of the way, or especially heroic - not all have the opportunity of heroic acts, of sufferings - but it means what the word perfection ordinarily means. By perfect we mean that which has no flaw in it, that which is complete, that which is consistent, that which is sound - we mean the opposite to imperfect. As we know well what imperfection in religious service means, we know by the contrast what is meant by perfection.[23]

Perfect love in the ordinary things

He, then, is perfect who does the work of the day perfectly, and we need not go beyond this to seek for perfection. You need not go out of the round of the day.[24]

Ordinary daily mortification

I would not have you go to any mortifications. I will tell you what the greatest mortification is: to do well the ordinary duties of the day. Determine to rise at a certain hour - to go through certain devotions... Don't oppress yourself with them, but keep to your rules - and you will find it a sufficient trial.[25]

Christian joy

Gloom is no Christian temper; that repentance is not real, which has not love in it; that self-chastisement is not acceptable which is not sweetened by faith and cheerfulness. We must live in sunshine, even when in sorrow; we must live in God's presence, we must not shut ourselves up in our own hearts, even when we are reckoning up our past sins.[26]

Christian peace

The foundations of the ocean, the vast realms of water which girdle the earth, are as tranquil and as silent in the storm as in a calm. So it is with the souls of holy men. They have a well of peace springing up within them unfathomable; and though the accidents of the hour may make them seem agitated, yet in their hearts they are not so.[27]

Living in the World

The deadening effect of love of this world

Bad as it is to be languid and indifferent in our secular duties, and to account this religion, yet it is far worse to be the slaves of this world, and to have our hearts in the concerns of this world. I do not know anything more dreadful than a state of mind which is, perhaps, the characteristic of this country, and which the prosperity of this country so miserably fosters. I mean that... low ambition which sets everyone on the look-out to succeed and to rise in life, to amass money, to gain power..., an intense, sleepless, restless, never wearied, never satisfied, pursuit of mammon in one shape or other, to the exclusion of all deep, all holy, all calm, all reverent thoughts.[28]

You cannot serve God and money

A smooth and easy life, an uninterrupted enjoyment of the goods of providence, full meals, soft raiment, well-furnished homes, the pleasures of sense, the feeling of security, the consciousness of wealth - these and the like, if we are not careful, choke up all the avenues of the soul through which the light and breath of heaven might come to us.[29]

∞

Assess the world with the eyes of faith

There are ten thousand ways of looking at this world, but only one right way. The man of pleasure has his way, the man of gain his, and the man of intellect his. Poor men and rich men, governors and governed, prosperous and discontented, learned and unlearned, each has his own way of looking at the things which come before him, and each has a wrong way. There is but one right way; it is the way in which God looks at the world. Aim at looking at it in God's way. Aim at seeing things as God sees them. Aim at forming judgments about persons, events, ranks, fortunes, changes, objects, such as God forms. Aim at looking at this life as God looks at it. Aim at looking at the life to come, and the world unseen as God does. Aim at seeing the king in his beauty. All things that we see are but shadows to us, and delusions, unless we enter into what they really mean.[30]

∞

All that is good comes from God

Even where there is habitual rebellion against him [God], or profound far-spreading social depravity, still the undercurrent, or the heroic outburst, of natural virtue, as well as the yearnings of the heart after what it has not, and its presentiment of its true remedies, are to be ascribed to the author of all good... All that is good, all that is true, all that is beautiful, all that is beneficent, be it great or small, be it perfect or fragmentary, natural as well as supernatural, moral as well as material, comes from him.[31]

Christ came to make a new world

He came into the world to regenerate it in himself, to make a new beginning, to be the beginning of the creation of God, to gather together in one, and recapitulate all things in himself. The rays of his glory were scattered through the world; one state of life had some of them, another others. The world was like some fair mirror, broken in pieces, and giving back no one uniform image of its maker. But he came to combine what was dissipated, to recast what was shattered in himself. He began all excellence, and of his fullness have we all received.[32]

How to use our intellect

I say that a cultivated intellect, because it is a good in itself, brings with it a power and a grace to every work and occupation which it undertakes, and enables us to be more useful, and to a greater number. There is a duty we owe to human society as such, to the state to which we belong, to the sphere in which we move.[33]

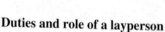

Duties and role of a layperson

I want an intelligent, well-instructed laity. I wish you to enlarge your knowledge, to cultivate your reason, to understand how faith and reason stand to each other, what are the bases and principles of Catholicism.[34]

Treat knowledge carefully

Knowledge, viewed as knowledge, exerts a subtle influence in throwing us back on ourselves, and making us our own centre, and our own minds the measure of all things.[35]

The dangers of pretence and hypocrisy

It is well to have a cultivated intellect, a delicate taste, a candid, equitable, dispassionate mind, a noble and courteous bearing in the conduct of life; these are the co-natural qualities of a large knowledge... they look like virtue at a distance, but they are detected by close observers, and in the long run; and hence it is that they are popularly accused of pretence and hypocrisy, not, I repeat, from their own fault, but because their professors and their admirers persist in taking them for what they are not, and are officious in arrogating for them a praise to which they have no claim. Quarry the granite rock with razors, or moor the vessel with a thread of silk; then you may hope with such keen and delicate instruments as human knowledge and human reason to contest against those giants, the passion and the pride of man.[36]

∽

Young people facing the world about them

We have most of us by nature longings more or less, and aspirations, after something greater than this world can give. Youth, especially has a natural love of what is noble and heroic. We like to hear marvellous tales, which throw us out of things as

they are, and introduce us to things that are not. We
so love the idea of the invisible that we even build
fabrics in the air for ourselves, if heavenly truth be
not vouchsafed us. We love to fancy ourselves
involved in circumstances of danger or trial, and
acquitting ourselves well under them. Or we imagine
some perfection, such as earth has not, which we
follow, and render it our homage and our heart. Such
is the state more or less of young persons before the
world alters them, before the world comes upon
them, as it often does very soon, with its polluting,
withering, debasing, deadening influence, before it
breathes on them, and blights and parches, and strips
off their green foliage, and leaves there, as dry and
wintry trees without sap or sweetness. But in early
youth we stand with our leaves and blossoms on
which promise fruit; we stand by the side of the still
waters, with our hearts beating high, with longings
after our unknown good, and with a sort of contempt
for the fashions of the world; with a contempt for the
world, even though we engage in it...[37]

∞

Christ gives what the world can never give

I am speaking of men ..., before they have given
their hearts to the world, which promises them true
good, then cheats them, and then makes them

believe there is no truth anywhere, and that they were fools for thinking it. But before that time they have desires after things above this world, which they embody in some form of this world, because they have no other way at all of realizing them. If they are in humble life, they dream of becoming their own masters, rising in the world, and securing an independence; if in a higher rank, they have ambitious thoughts of gaining a name and exercising power. While their hearts are thus unsettled, Christ comes to them, if they will receive him, and promises to satisfy their great need, this hunger and thirst which wearies them. He does not wait till they have learned to ridicule high feelings as mere romantic dreams: he comes to the young; he has them baptised betimes, and then promises them, and in a higher way, those unknown blessings which they yearn after.[38]

Developing my Faith

True discernment

Beware of trifling with your conscience. It is often said that second thoughts are best; so they are in matters of judgment, but not in matters of conscience. In matters of duty first thoughts are commonly best - they have more in them of the voice of God.[39]

The desire and gift of a clear conscience

Many is the time when they cannot tell how much that true inward guide commands, and how much comes from a mere earthly source. So that the gift of conscience raises a desire for what it does not itself fully supply... It creates in them a thirst, an impatience, for the knowledge of that unseen Lord, and governor and judge, who as yet speaks to them only secretly, who whispers in their hearts, who tells them something, but not nearly so much as they wish and as they need. Thus... a religious man, who has not the blessing of the infallible teaching of revelation, is led to look out for it.[40]

Developing your conscience

Certainly I have always contended that obedience, even to an erring conscience was the way to gain light, and that it mattered not where a man began, so that he began on what came to hand, and in faith; and that any thing might become a divine method of truth; that to the pure all things are pure, and have a self-correcting virtue and a power of germinating.[41]

~

Can my reason inform my faith?

There is a difficulty in doubting: a difficulty in determining there is no truth; in saying that there is a truth, but that no-one can find it out; in saying that all religious opinions are true, or one as good as another; a difficulty in saying there is no God; that there is a God but that he has not revealed himself except in the way of nature; and there is doubtless a difficulty in Christianity. The question is, whether on the whole our reason does not tell us that it is a duty to accept the arguments commonly urged for its truth as sufficient, and a duty in consequence to believe heartily in scripture and the Church.[42]

~

Can intuition help my faith?

A nother thought which I wish to put before you is, whether our nature does not tell us that there is something which has more intimate relations with the question of religion than intellectual exercises have, and that is our conscience. We have the idea of duty - duty suggests something or someone to which it is to be referred, to which we are responsible. That something that has dues upon us is to us God. I will not assume it is a personal God, or that it is more than a law (though of course I hold that it is the living seeing God) but still the idea of duty, and the terrible anguish of conscience, and the irrepressible distress and confusion of face which the transgression of what we believe to be our duty, cause us, all this is an intimation, a clear evidence, that there is something nearer to religion than intellect; and that, if there is a way of finding religious truth, it lies, not in exercises of intellect, but close on the side of duty, of conscience, in the observance of the moral law. Now all this may seem a truism, and many an intellectualist will say that he grants it freely. But I think that, when dwelt upon, it leads to conclusions which would both surprise and annoy him.[43]

Role of my intellect and my faith

You must not suppose that I am denying the intellect its real place in the discovery of truth, but it must ever be borne in mind that its exercise mainly consists of reasoning - that is, in comparing things, classifying them, and inferring. It ever needs points to start from, first principles, and these it does not provide - but it can no more move one step without these starting points, than a stick, which supports a man, can move without the man's action... To gain religious starting points, we must interrogate our hearts, and (since it is a personal, individual matter) our own hearts – interrogate our own consciences, interrogate, I will say, the God who dwells there.[44]

Grounds for being a Catholic

I am a Catholic by virtue of my believing in a God; and if I am asked why I believe in a God, I answer that it is because I believe in myself, for I feel it impossible to believe in my own existence (and of that fact I am quite sure) without believing also in the existence of him, who lives as a personal, all-seeing, all-judging being in my conscience.[45]

The objective reality of the Church

In the Catholic Church... I recognised at once a reality which was quite a new thing with me. Then I was sensible that I was not making for myself a Church by an effort of thought; I needed not to make an act of faith in her; I had not painfully to force myself into a position, but my mind fell back upon itself in relaxation and peace, and I gazed at her almost passively as a great objective fact. I looked at her at her rites, her ceremonial and her precepts, and I said, 'This is a religion'.[46]

I am part of the body of Christ

This then is the special glory of the Christian Church, that its members do not depend merely on what is visible, they are not mere stones of a building, piled one on another, and bound together from without, but they are, one and all, the births and manifestations of one and the same unseen spiritual principle of power, 'living stones' internally connected, as branches from a tree, not as the parts of a heap. They are members of the body of Christ.[47]

We are united in prayer

Christians could not correspond; they could not combine but they could pray for one another. Even their public prayers partook of this character of intercession; for to pray for the welfare of the whole Church was in fact a prayer for all classes of men and all individuals of which it was composed. It was in prayer that the Church was founded.[47a]

Human love inspired by divine love

We find our Saviour had a private friend; and this shows us, first, how entirely he was a man, as much as any of us, in his wants and feelings; and next, that there is nothing contrary to the spirit of the Gospel, nothing inconsistent with the fullness of Christian love, in having our affections directed in an especial way towards certain objects, towards those whom the circumstances of our past life, or some peculiarities of character, have endeared to us.[48]

Love one another as I have loved you

There have been men before now, who have supposed Christian love was so diffusive as not to admit of concentration upon individuals; so that we ought to love all men equally. And many there are, who, without bringing forward any theory, yet consider practically that the love of many is something superior to the love of one or two; and neglect the charities of private life while busy in the schemes of an expansive benevolence, or of effecting a general union and conciliation among Christians. Now I shall here maintain, in opposition to such notions of Christian love, and with our Saviour's pattern before me, that the best preparation for loving the world at large, and loving it duly and wisely, is to cultivate an intimate friendship and affection towards those who are immediately about us.[49]

Our love must be real and not just words

We are to begin with loving our friends about us, and gradually to enlarge the circle of our affections, till it reaches all Christians, and then all men... We see then how absurd it is, when writers... talk magnificently about loving the whole human race with a comprehensive affection, of being friends of all mankind; this is not to love men, it is but to talk of love. The real love of man must depend on practice.[50]

Relating to other Christians

Every one who desires unity, who prays for it, who endeavours to further it, who witnesses for it, who behaves Christianly towards the members of Churches alienated from us, who is at amity with them (saving his duty to his own communion and to the truth itself), who tries to edify them, while he edifies himself and his own people, may surely be considered, as far as he himself is concerned, as breaking down the middle wall of division, and renewing the ancient bonds of unity and concord by the power of charity.[51]

As a faithful member of the Church

I think certainly that the teaching Church is more happy when she has enthusiastic partisans about her... than when she cuts off the faithful from the study of her divine doctrines and the sympathy of her divine contemplations, and she requires from them an implicit faith in her word, which in the educated classes will terminate in indifference, and in the poorer in superstition.[52]

⊙⊷✝⊶⊙

Living as a True Witness

Our prayers open heaven to the world

Let us but raise the level of religion in our hearts and it will rise in the world. He who attempts to set up God's Kingdom in his heart, furthers it in the world. He whose prayers come up for a memorial before God, opens the windows of heaven, and the foundations of the great deep, and the waters rise.[53]

How can I be a witness to Christ?

Stay with me, and then I shall begin to shine as thou shinest: so to shine as to be a light to others. The light, O Jesus, will be all from thee. None of it will be mine. No merit to me. It will be thou who shinest through me upon others. O let me thus praise thee, in the way which thou dost love best, by shining on all those around me. Give light to them as well as to me; light them with me, through me. Teach me to show forth thy praise, thy truth, thy will. Make me preach thee without preaching - not by words, but by my example and by the catching force, the sympathetic influence, of what I do - by my visible resemblance to thy saints, and the evident fullness of the love which my heart bears to thee.[54]

᎒᎒

Preaching the Good News

Christianity is eminently an objective religion. For the most part it tells us of persons and facts in simple words, and leaves that announcement to produce its effect on such hearts as are prepared to receive it.[55]

᎒᎒

The power of the preaching

Definiteness is the life of preaching. A definite hearer, not the whole world; a definite topic, not the whole evangelical tradition; and, in like manner, a definite speaker. Nothing that is anonymous will preach; nothing that is dead and gone; nothing even which is of yesterday, however religious in itself and useful. Thought and word are one in the Eternal Logos, and must not be separate in those who are his shadows on earth. They must issue fresh and fresh, as from the preacher's mouth, so from his breast, if they are to be 'spirit and life' to the hearts of his hearers.[56]

᎒᎒

How can I speak about my religion?

What I have been saying comes to this - be in earnest, and you will speak of religion where, and when, and how you should; aim at things, and your words will be right without aiming.[57]

Easter's promise of innocence

I recollect well my own thoughts and feelings, as I lay in my crib in the early spring, with outdoor scents, sounds and sights wakening me up, and especially the cheerful ring of the mower's scythe on the lawn, which Milton long before me had noted; - and how in coming down stairs slowly, for I brought down both feet on each step, I said to myself 'This is June!' though what my particular experience of June was, and how it was broad enough to be a matter of reflection I really cannot tell... May the day come for all of us, of which Easter is the promise, when that first spring may return to us, and a sweetness which cannot die may gladden our garden.[58]

God's footsteps in our personal history

Such are the feelings with which men often look back on their childhood, when any accident brings it vividly before them. Some relic or token of that early time, some spot, or some book, or a word or a scent, or a sound, brings them back in memory to the first years of their discipleship, and they then see, what they could not know at the time, that God's presence went up with them and gave them rest. Nay, even now perhaps they are unable to discern fully what it was which made that time so bright and glorious. They are full of tender and affectionate thoughts towards those first years, but they do not know why. They think it is those very years which they yearn after, whereas it is the presence of God which, as they now see, was then over them, which attracts them.[59]

How much Christ has loved me

Now I bid you consider that that face, so ruthlessly smitten, was the face of God himself; the brows bloody with the thorns, the sacred body exposed to view and lacerated with the scourge, the hands nailed to the cross, and, afterwards, the side pierced with the spear; it was the blood, and the sacred flesh, and the hands, and the temples, and the side, and the feet of God himself, which the frenzied multitude then gazed upon.[60]

God's mercy for me

Christ's work of mercy has two chief parts; what he did for all men, what he does for each; what he did once for all, what he does for one by one continually; what he did externally to us, what he does within us; what he did on earth, what he does in heaven; what he did in his own person, what he does by his Spirit.[60a]

The Holy Spirit is my defender

No one, doubtless, can deny this most gracious and consolatory truth that the Holy Ghost is come; but why has he come? To supply Christ's absence, or to accomplish his presence? Surely to make him present. Let us not for a moment suppose that God the Holy Ghost comes in such sense that God the Son remains away. No, he has not so come that Christ does not come, but rather he comes that Christ may come in his coming. Through the Holy Ghost we have communion with the Father and the Son.[61]

Christ's love for the lonely

Let all those who are in trouble take this comfort to themselves, if they are trying to lead a spiritual

life. If they call on God, he will answer them.
Though they have no earthly friend, they have him,
who, as he felt for his mother when he was on the
cross, now that he is in his glory, feels for the lowest
and feeblest of his people.[62]

Come Holy Spirit, come to me

Thou alone canst fill the soul of man, and thou
hast promised to do so. Thou art the living flame,
and ever burnest with love of man: enter into me
and set me on fire after thy pattern and likeness.[63]

Mary is my mother

Mary is exalted for the sake of Jesus. It was
fitting that she, as being a creature, though the
first of creatures, should have an office of
ministration. She, as others, came into the world to
do a work, she had a mission to fulfil; her grace and
her glory are not for her own sake but for her
maker's; and to her is committed the custody of the
incarnation... her glories and the devotion paid her
proclaim and define the right faith concerning him
as God and man.[64]

∞✝∞

True Christian Wisdom

The wisdom that comes with age

As time goes on you will know yourself better and better. Time does that for us, not only by the increase of experience, but by the withdrawal of those natural assistances to devotion and self-surrender which youth furnishes. When the spirits are high and the mind fervent, though we may have waywardness and perverseness which we have not afterwards, yet we have something to battle against them. But when men get old... then they see how little grace is in them, and how much what seemed grace was but nature.[65]

∞

Accepting our true poverty

With old age the soul is left to lassitude, torpor, dejection and coldness which is its real state, with no natural impulses, affections or imaginations to rouse it and things which in youth seemed easy then become difficult. Then it finds how little self command it has, and how little it can throw off the tempter when he comes behind and places it in a certain direction or position, or throws it down, or places his foot upon it. Then it understands at length its own nothingness, and that it has less grace than it had but it has nothing but grace to aid it. It is the sign of a saint to grow; common minds, even though they are in the grace of God, dwindle, (i.e. seem to do so) as time goes on.[66]

In old age turn to Mary

The energy of grace alone can make a soul strong in age. Do not then be cast down, if you though not very aged feel less fervent than you did ten years since - only let it be a call on you to seek grace to supply nature, as well as to overcome it. Put yourself ever fully and utterly into Mary's hands and she will nurse you and bring you forward. She will watch over you as a mother over a sick child.[67]

Time passes relentlessly on

There is something awful in the silent resistless sweep of time - and, as years go on, and friends are taken away, one draws the thought of those who remain about one, as in cold weather one buttons up great coats and capes, for protection.[68]

The lives of saints

A saint's writings are to me his real 'Life'... Perhaps I shall be asked what I mean by 'Life'. I mean a narrative which impresses the reader with the idea of moral unity, identity, growth, continuity, personality. When a saint converses with me, I am conscious of the presence of one active principle of thought, one individual character, flowing on and into the various matters which he discusses, and the different transactions in which he mixes. It is what no memorials can reach, however skillfully elaborated, however free from effort or study, however conscientiously faithful, however guaranteed by the veracity of the writers. Why cannot art rival the lily or the rose? Because the colours of the flower are developed and blended by the force of an inward life; while on the other hand, the lights and shades of the painter are diligently laid on from without... When I read St Augustine or St Basil, I hold converse with a beautiful, grace-illumined soul, looking out into this world of sense, and leavening it with itself; when I read a professed life of him, I am wandering in a labyrinth of which I cannot find the centre and heart, and am but conducted out of doors again when I do my best to penetrate within.[69]

Carry your cross every day

Year passes after year, silently; Christ's coming is ever nearer than it was. O that, as he comes nearer earth we may approach nearer heaven! O my brethren, pray him to give you the heart to seek him in sincerity. Pray him to make you in earnest. You have one work only, to bear your cross after him. Resolve in his strength to do so. Resolve to be no longer beguiled by shadows of religion, by words, or by disputings, or by notions, or by high professions, or by excuses, or by the world's promises or threats.[70]

Perfection through obedience to God

Pray him to give you what Scripture calls 'an honest or good heart', or a 'perfect heart', and, without waiting, begin at once to obey him with the best heart you have. Any obedience is better than none - any profession which is disjoined from obedience, is a mere pretence and deceit. Any religion which does not bring you nearer to God is of the world. You have to seek his face; obedience is the only way of seeking him. All your duties are obediences. If you are to believe the truths he has revealed, to regulate yourselves by his precepts, to be frequent in his ordinances, to adhere to his

Church and people, why is it, except because he has
bid you? And to do what he bids is to obey him, and
to obey him is to approach him.[71]

∽

Life is short and death is certain

Every act of obedience is an approach - an
approach to him who is not far off, though he
seems so, but close behind this visible screen of
things which hides him from us. He is behind this
material framework; earth and sky are but a veil
going between him and us; the day will come when
he will rend that veil, and show himself to us. And
then, according as we have waited for him, will he
recompense us. If we have forgotten him, he will not
know us, but 'blessed are those servants whom the
Lord, when he cometh, shall find watching... he shall
gird himself, and make them sit down to meat, and
will come forth and serve them. And if he shall come
in the second watch, or come in the third watch, and
find them so, blessed are those servants'. May this be
the portion of every one of us! It is hard to attain it;
but it is woeful to fail. Life is short; death is certain;
and the world to come is everlasting.[72]

∽

Understand the power of God in nature

Once only in the year, yet once, does the world which we see show forth its hidden powers, and in a manner manifest itself. Then the leaves come out, and the blossoms on the fruit trees and flowers; and the grass and corn spring up. There is a sudden rush and burst outwardly of that hidden life which God has lodged in the material world. Well, that shows you as by a sample, what it can do at God's command, when he gives the word. This earth, which now buds forth in leaves and blossoms, will one day burst forth into a new world of light and glory, in which we shall see saints and angels dwelling. Who would think, except from his experience of former springs all through his life, who could conceive two or three months before, that it was possible that the face of nature, which then seemed so lifeless, should become so splendid and varied?[73]

The end is coming and with it the Kingdom

So it is with the coming of that Eternal Spring for which all Christians are waiting. Come it will, though it delay; yet though it tarry, let us wait for it, 'because it will surely come, it will not tarry'. Therefore we say day by day, 'Thy Kingdom come,' which means, 'O Lord, show thyself; manifest thyself; thou that sittest between the cherubim, show thyself; stir up thy strength and come and help us.' (*Ps* 80) The earth that we see does not satisfy us. What we see is the outward shell of an eternal kingdom; and on that kingdom we fix the eyes of our faith.[74]

∽

What do I think about dying?

Looking beyond this life, my first prayer, aim and hope is that I may see God. The thought of being blest with the sight of earthly friends pales before that thought. I believe that I shall never die; this awful prospect would crush me, were it not that I trusted and prayed that it would be an eternity in God's presence. How is eternity a boon unless he goes with it? And for others dear to me, my one prayer is that they may see God.[75]

∽

Living in eternity

Thou, O my God, art ever new, though thou art the most ancient thou alone art the food for eternity. I am to live for ever, not for a time - and I have no power over my being; I cannot destroy myself, even though I were so wicked as to wish to do so. I must live on, with intellect and consciousness for ever, in spite of myself. Without thee eternity would be another name for eternal misery. In thee alone have I that which can stay me up for ever; thou alone art the food of my soul. Thou alone art inexhaustible, and ever offerest to me something new to know, something new to love...and so on for eternity I shall ever be a little child beginning to be taught the rudiments of thy infinite divine nature. For thou art thyself the seat and centre of all good, and the only substance in this universe of shadows, and the heaven in which blessed spirits live and rejoice - Amen.[76]

Peace at the last

May he support us all the day long, till the shades lengthen, and the evening comes, and the busy world is hushed, and the fever of life is over, and our work is done. Then in his mercy may he give us a safe lodging, and a holy rest, and peace at the last.[77]

An Ethical Character

Hence it is that it is almost a definition of a gentleman to say he is one who never inflicts pain. This description is both refined and, as far as it goes, accurate. He is mainly occupied in merely removing the obstacles which hinder the free and unembarrassed action of those about him; and he concurs with their movements rather than takes the initiative himself. His benefits may be considered as parallel to what are called comforts or conveniences in arrangements of a personal nature; like an easy-chap or a good fire, which do their part in dispelling cold and fatigue, though nature provides both means of rest and animal heat without them.[78]

Gentle

The true gentleman in like manner carefully avoids whatever may cause a jar or a jolt in the minds of those with whom he is cast, all dashing of opinion, or collision of feeling, all restraint, or suspicion, or gloom, or resentment; his great concern being to make everyone at their ease and at home.

He has his eyes on all his company; he is tender towards the bashful, gentle towards the distant, and merciful towards the absurd; he can recollect to whom he is speaking; he guards against unseasonable allusions or topics which may irritate; he is seldom prominent in conversation and never wearisome. He makes light of favours while he does them, and seems to be receiving when he is conferring. He never speaks of himself except when counselled, never defends himself by a mere retort; he has no ears for slander or gossip, is scrupulous in imputing motives to those who interfere with him, and interprets everything for the best. He is never mean or little in his disputes, never takes unfair advantage, never mistakes personalities or sharp sayings for arguments, or insinuates evil which he dare not say out.[79]

⌀

Prudent

From a long-sighted prudence, he observes the maxim of the ancient sage, that we should ever conduct ourselves towards our enemy as if he were one day to be our friend. He has too much good sense to be affronted at insults, he is too well employed to remember injuries, and too indolent to

bear malice. He is patient, forbearing, and resigned,
on philosophical principles; he submits to pain,
because it is inevitable, to bereavement, because it is
irreparable, and to death, because it is his destiny. If
he engages in controversy of any kind, his
disciplined intellect preserves hire from the
blundering discourtesy of better, perhaps, 'but less
educated minds, who, like blunt weapons, tear and
hack instead of cutting clean, who mistake the point
in argument, waste their strength on trifles,
misconceive their adversary, and leave the question
more involved than they find it. He may be right or
wrong in his opinion, but he is too clear-headed to
be unjust, he is as simple as he is forcible, and as
brief as he is decisive.[80]

Respectful

Nowhere shall we find greater candour,
consideration, indulgence; he throws himself into
the minds of his opponents, he accounts for their
mistakes. He knows the weakness of human reason
as well as its strength, its province and its limits. If he
be an unbeliever, he will be too profound and large-
minded to ridicule religion or to act against it; he is
too wise to be a dogmatist or fanatic in his infidelity.

He respects piety and devotion; he even supports institutions as venerable, beautiful, or useful, to which he does not assent; he honours the ministers of religion, and it contents him to decline its mysteries without assailing or denouncing them. He is a friend of religious toleration and that, not only because his philosophy has taught him to look on all forms of faith with an impartial eye, but also from the gentleness and effeminacy of feeling, which is the attendant on civilization.[81]

Religious

Not that he may not hold a religion too, in his own way, even when he is not a Christian. In that case his religion is one of imagination and sentiment; it is the embodiment of those ideas of the sublime, majestic, and beautiful, without which there can be no large philosophy. Sometimes he acknowledges the being of God; sometimes he invests an unknown principle or quality with the attributes of perfection. Such are some of the lineaments of the ethical character, which the cultivated intellect will form, apart from religious principle.[82]

Hymns and Prayers

Praise to the holiest in the height

Praise to the holiest in the height;
And in the depth be praise:
In all his words most wonderful;
Most sure in all his ways.

O loving wisdom of our God!
When all was sin and shame,
A second Adam to the fight
And to the rescue came.

O wisest love! that flesh and blood
Which did in Adam fail,
Should strive afresh against the foe,
Should strive and should prevail;

And that a higher gift than grace
Should flesh and blood refine,
God's presence and his very self,
And essence all divine.

O generous love! that he who smote
In man for man the foe,

The double agony in man
For man should undergo.

And in the garden secretly
And on the cross on high,
Should teach his brethren and inspire
To suffer and to die.[83]

Anima Christi

Soul of Christ, be my sanctification;
Body of Christ, be my salvation;
Blood of Christ, fill all my veins;
Water of Christ's side, wash out my stains;
Passion of Christ, my comfort be;
O good Jesu, listen to me;
In thy wounds I fain would hide,
Ne'er to be parted from thy side;
Guard me, should the foe assail me;
Call me when my life shall fail me,
Bid me come to thee above,
With thy saints to sing thy love,
World without end. Amen.[84]

Lead kindly light

Lead, kindly light, amid the encircling gloom,
Lead thou me on!
The night is dark, and I am far from home, -
Lead thou me on!
Keep thou my feet; I do not ask to see
The distant scene, - one step enough for me.

It was not ever thus, nor pray'd that thou
Shouldst lead me on.
I loved to choose and see my path, but now
Lead thou me on!
I loved the garish day, and spite of fears,
Pride ruled my will: remember not past years.

So long thy power hath blest me, sure it still
Will lead me on,
O'er moor and fen, o'er crag and torrent, till
The night is gone;
And with the morn those angel faces smile
Which I have lov'd long since, and lost awhile.[85]

The last things

Jesu, Maria - I am near to death,
And thou art calling me; I know it now,
Not by the token of this faltering breath,

This chill at heart, this dampness on my brow, -
(Jesu, have mercy! Mary, pray for me!)
'Tis this new feeling, never felt before,
(Be with me, Lord, in my extremity!)
That I am going, that I am no more,
'Tis this strange innermost abandonment
(Lover of souls! great God! I look to thee,)
This emptying out of each constituent
And natural force, by which I come to be.
Pray for me, O my friends; a visitant
Is knocking his dire summons at my door,
The like of whom, to scare me and to daunt,
Has never, never come to me before.[86]

Raised from the dead

Take me away, and in the lowest deep
     There let me be,
And there in hope the lone night-watches keep,
Told out for me.
There, motionless and happy in my pain,
Lone, not forlorn, -
There will I sing my sad perpetual strain,
Until the morn.
There will I sing, and soothe my stricken breast,
Which ne'er can cease

To throb, and pine, and languish, till possest
Of its sole peace.
There will I sing my absent Lord and Love: -
Take me away
That sooner I may rise, and go above,
And see him in the truth of everlasting day.[87]

Notes

1. Parochial and Plain Sermons
2. Meditations and Devotions
3. Meditations and Devotions
4. Letter, October 1873
5. Parochial and Plain Sermons
6. Parochial and Plain Sermons
7. Letter, April 1853
8. Meditations and Devotions
9. Parochial and Plain Sermons
10. Essay on the Development of Christian Doctrine
11. Essay on Development
12. Parochial and Plain Sermons
13. Meditations and Devotions
14. Discourses Addressed to Mixed Congregations
15. Parochial and Plain Sermons
16. Fifteen Sermons preached before the University of Oxford
17. Parochial and Plain Sermons
18. Parochial and Plain Sermons
19. Parochial and Plain Sermons
20. Parochial and Plain Sermons
21. Letter, July 1853
22. Meditations and Devotions
23. Meditations and Devotions
24. Meditations and Devotions
25. Letter, December 1850
26. Parochial and Plain Sermons
27. Parochial and Plain Sermons
28. Parochial and Plain Sermons
29. Parochial and Plain Sermons

30. Parochial and Plain Sermons
31. Idea of a University
32. Sermons bearing on Subjects of the Day
33. Idea of a University
34. Present Position of Catholics in England
35. Idea of a University
36. Idea of a University
37. Parochial and Plain Sermons
38. Parochial and Plain Sermons
39. Parochial and Plain Sermons
40. Sermons Preached on Various Occasions
41. Apologia
42. Letter, June 1869
43. Letter, June 1869
44. Letter, June 1869
45. Apologia
46. Apologia
47. Parochial and Plain Sermons
47a Certain Difficulties Felt by Anglicans in Catholic Teaching
48. Parochial and Plain Sermons
49. Parochial and Plain Sermons
50. Parochial and Plain Sermons
51. Essays Critical and Historical
52. On Consulting the Faithful in Matters of doctrine
53. Parochial and Plain Sermons
54. Meditations and Devotions
55. Essay on Development
56. Idea of a University
57. Parochial and Plain Sermons
58. Letter, April 1876

59. Parochial and Plain Sermons
60. Parochial and Plain Sermons
60a Lectures on the Doctrine of Justification
61. Parochial and Plain Sermons
62. Meditations and Devotions
63. Meditations and Devotions
64. Discourses Addressed to Mixed Congregations
65. Letter, July 1850
66. Letter, July 1850
67. Letter, July 1850
68. Letter, January 1860
69. Historical Sketches, Vol. 2
70. Parochial and Plain Sermons
71. Parochial and Plain Sermons
72. Parochial and Plain Sermons
73. Parochial and Plain Sermons
74. Parochial and Plain Sermons
75. Letter, February 1880
76. Meditations and Devotions
77. Sermons bearing on Subjects of the Day
78. Idea of a University
79. Idea of a University
80. Idea of a University
81. Idea of a University
82. Idea of a University
83. Dream of Gerontius
84. Newman's translation of Anima Christi
85. The Pillar of the Cloud
86. Dream of Gerontius
87. Dream of Gerontius

Acknowledgement: This collection of sayings, meditations and prayers has been drawn from a larger work first published by the CTS in 1987: *Guides to Holiness, John Henry Newman*, edited by Joyce Sugg.